Little Helpers

Mary Rose

Name _____

Age _____

Class _____

OXFORD
UNIVERSITY PRESS

OXFORD
UNIVERSITY PRESS

Great Clarendon Street, Oxford OX2 6DP

Oxford University Press is a department of the University of Oxford.
It furthers the University's objective of excellence in research, scholarship,
and education by publishing worldwide in

Oxford New York

Auckland Cape Town Dar es Salaam Hong Kong Karachi
Kuala Lumpur Madrid Melbourne Mexico City Nairobi
New Delhi Shanghai Taipei Toronto

With offices in

Argentina Austria Brazil Chile Czech Republic France Greece
Guatemala Hungary Italy Japan South Korea Poland Portugal
Singapore Switzerland Thailand Turkey Ukraine Vietnam

OXFORD and OXFORD ENGLISH are registered trade marks of
Oxford University Press in the UK and in certain other countries

© Oxford University Press 2005

ISBN 978 0 19 440083 1

Printed in China

Illustrations by: Cathy Hughes/Beehive Illustrations
With thanks to Sally Spray for her contribution to this series

Reading Dolphins
Notes for teachers & parents

📖 Using the book

1 Begin by looking at the first story page (page 2). Look at the picture and ask questions about it. Then read the story text under the picture with your students. Use section 1 of the CD for this if possible.

2 Teach and check the understanding of any new vocabulary. Note that some of the words are in the **Picture Dictionary** at the back of the book.

3 Now look at the activities on the right-hand page. Show the example to the students and instruct them to complete the activities. This may be done individually, in pairs, or as a class.

4 Do the same for the remaining pages of the book.

5 Retell the whole story more quickly, reinforcing the new vocabulary. Sections 2 and 3 of the CD can help with this.

6 If possible, listen to the expanded story (section 4 of the CD). The students should follow in their books.

7 When the book is finished, use the **Picture Dictionary** to check that students understand and remember new vocabulary. Section 5 of the CD can help with this.

💿 Using the CD

The CD contains five sections.

1 The story told slowly, with pauses. Use this during the first reading. It may also be used for "Listen and repeat" activities at any point.

2 The story told at normal speed. This should be used once the students have read the book for the first time.

3 The story chanted. Students may want to chant along with the story.

4 The expanded story. The story is told in a longer version. This will help the students understand English when it is spoken faster, as they will now know the story and the vocabulary.

5 Vocabulary. Each word in the **Picture Dictionary** is spoken and then used in a simple sentence.

This is Tom.
He helps his mother
in the kitchen.

1 Trace and write.

jam   jam   jam

rice

flour

2 Connect.

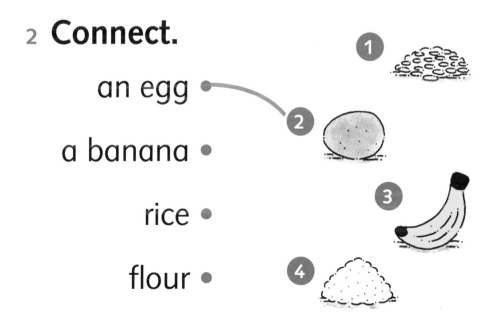

an egg •

a banana •

rice •

flour •

Amy is a good girl.
She helps her father
to wash the car.

Number.

6 Amy washes the car.

☐ Amy washes a wheel.

☐ Amy washes a seat.

☐ Amy washes the window.

☐ Amy washes a door.

☐ Amy washes her dog.

Can you see Mark?
He helps his grandmother
at the supermarket.

Connect.

eggs

chocolate

oranges

cookies

tea

rice

sugar

bananas

1
2
3
4
5
6
7
8

Look at Julie.
She helps her grandfather
in the mountains.

Trace and write.

rope   rope

rock

head

hand

hat

David is a helper.
He helps his brother
on his bicycle.

1 Connect.

bicycle •
duck •
cat •
wheel •
dog •

2 Trace and write.

cat   cat   cat   cat

duck

bicycle

11

This is Emily.
She helps her big sister
with her picture.

1 Connect.

red •   1 2 • yellow

blue •   3 4 • purple

green •   5 6 • orange

2 Trace and write.

red   red   red

blue

green

We are all helpers.
Can we help you?

Connect.

Mark •   • Emily

Tom •   • Julie

David •   • Amy

Picture Dictionary

banana

duck

bicycle

egg

blue

flour

car

green

chocolate

jam

cookie

orange

purple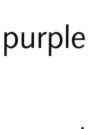

seat

red

sugar

rice

tea

rock

wheel

rope

yellow

Dolphin Readers

Dolphin Readers are available at five levels, from Starter to 4.

The Dolphins series covers four major themes:

Grammar, Living Together, The World Around Us, Science and Nature.

For each theme, there are two titles at every level.

Activity Books are available for all Dolphins.

All Dolphins are available on audio CD.
(2 TITLES ON EACH CD 💿 SEE TABLE BELOW)

Teacher's Notes are available at **www.oup.com/elt/dolphins**

	Grammar	Living Together	The World Around Us	Science and Nature
Starter	• Silly Squirrel • Monkeying Around	• My Family • A Day with Baby	• Doctor, Doctor • Moving House	• A Game of Shapes • Baby Animals
Level 1	• Meet Molly • Where Is It?	• Little Helpers • Jack the Hero	• On Safari • Lost Kitten	• Number Magic • How's the Weather?
Level 2	• Double Trouble • Super Sam	• Candy for Breakfast • Lost!	• A Visit to the City • Matt's Mistake	• Numbers, Numbers Everywhere • Circles and Squares
Level 3	• Students in Space • What Did You Do Yesterday?	• New Girl in School • Uncle Jerry's Great Idea	• Just Like Mine • Wonderful Wild Animals	• Things That Fly • Let's Go to the Rainforest
Level 4	• The Tough Task • Yesterday, Today and Tomorrow	• We Won the Cup • Up and Down	• Where People Live • City Girl, Country Boy	• In the Ocean • Go, Gorillas, Go